THE POOL OF PARADISE
A 30 DAY CURRICULUM

Elizabeth Bootman

INTRODUCTION

This book is as a very simplified interpretation of the Conference of the Birds originally written in the 12th century by Farid ud-Din Attar.

It can be used as a teaching tool for the Holy Month of Ramadan and the 30 days of fasting or as a curriculum to help children contemplate how each of the 30 birds overcome challenges in their stories.

When God (swt) created the Will, it was found to be defiant and disobedient. After many failed trials, at last, the Will was placed in the Valley of Hunger and after 1,000 years of exile the Will recognized the Creator of All Things.

Some may be familiar with the fasting of Ramadan. They may be aware that those who practice this fast are hungry and thirsty but they may not know why they choose to engage in this practice. The Will gives many excuses for its disobedience but there are times when the Will can choose the Right Path. Harness the energy of courage to represent the struggle of the ego.

This text is written to accompany a project for Ramadan where the student adds a bird to the Pool of Paradise each day. Each bird is assigned a distinguishing character or aspect of their Will. Each bird is also assigned a phase of the moon in its progression.

It is hoped that at the end of this project the student will have a greater appreciation of the purpose of fasting and the Will that can be tamed and guided to a goal greater than its own satisfaction.

When the birds reach the Pool of Paradise on Mount Qaf they look into the silver pool at their mirror image. They have lost themselves along the way and are annihilated in their cause to reach the Simourgh. In the pool they see their True King and not themselves as their reflection.

With this image we wish to describe the concept of fanah or annihilation.

The language of the episodes is at times above the comprehension level of younger children so this can add to the lesson. The overall goal is for the student to have a sense that each bird is facing a challenge just as we are challenged by the fast each day of Ramadan.

Wherever possible in the narrative the stories of the prophets are used as examples.

INVOCATION

In the name of God (swt), Creator of the heavens and the earth.

We search for the Lord in the skies where we fly, the waters that we swim, the perches where we light.

The Prophets of God (swt) have come to teach us and all the other beings that light on this earth.

Gather my flock together and hear of the journey we will make to find Our Creator, Our Leader, Our Home.

Leave behind your comfort and fear and understanding to find what is Real and True.

THE HOOPOE ADDRESSES THE ASSEMBLY

"I have even been a faithful servant to my master Sulayman (as) and it is his master that we must seek. Leave your egos, leave your fears and come with me to find our True Master. It is the Simourgh that we seek yet when we find him you will see that only your soul can perceive him."

So one by one each bird took heart but once they heard of the trials before them they paused and doubted and so the Hoopoe said,

"When the creator regarded the Well of Souls before him and sent them out each to fulfill their quest He gave them a secret. This secret was given to help each defeat their greatest enemy and return victorious to the Creator. Now all of you who gather here have forgotten the Day of Promises and your secrets, know not your quest and follow your enemy like a tethered animal. When the creator made your souls he gave each soul its Will. The Will to do good or the Will to turn to evil. This Will is precious and it is what sets you apart from the Angels made before you. Your creator used many means to guide this Will and all but one failed. When your creator cast the Will into the Valley of Hunger it said "You are the One and True Lord and Creator and to You alone we turn." For thirty days we will travel on our journey. We will fight our fear, our anger and our hunger so that we may recognize the creator once more and leave the Valley of Hunger again. Our Creator has given us the gift of Ramadan so that each year we can remember Our Quest, Our Origin and Our Home.

NIGHTINGALE

The Nightingale sings each night the songs of Daoud,

But the nightingale thought only of its rose and not its thorns or the plant or the leaves or the roots or the earth, air and water.

The nightingale sang,

"Your love is better than life, my lips will glorify You. I will praise You as long as I live, and in Your Name I will lift up my hands. I think of you through the watches of the night. Because You are my help, I sing in the shadow of Your Wings. My soul clings to You; Your Right Hand upholds me.

"I will sing of Your Strength, in the morning I will sing of Your Love; for You are my fortress, my refuge in times of trouble. From the ends of the earth I call to You, I call as my heart grows faint; lead me to the rock that is higher than I, for You have been my refuge, a strong tower against the foe."

Behind the face of his beloved rose was the face of the One Who Created All. The nightingale said, "I am weak and cannot leave my illusions and seek the Creator of My Beloved."

LESSON PLAN

After reading the passage about the Nightingale your child will place the Nightingale medallion on the pool at the top and the birds that will follow will go the left so that they are moving counter clockwise around the pool.

Discussion questions: Why is the bird having difficulty to make the journey? What do you think the Hoopoe bird will say to convince the Nightingale to go on the journey?

HOOPOE

The Hoopoe addressed the Nightingale, pleading with him to not be deceived by the illusions of this world no matter how lovely and enchanting they may be. He begged the Nightingale to perceive the thorns and the wilting petals.

"If you lose your rose one day you will know that all that is beautiful comes from Our Lord and all that is false comes from ourselves. If you love only that which is mortal and fleeting you will always be disappointed and desolate, dear Nightingale, so follow me to the source of all that is beautiful and all that your heart can desire because there is but One Vessel that can contain the Creator: the heart that lies in your breast."

The nightingale lowered her head, submitted and followed the Hoopoe on the journey.

LESSON PLAN

After reading the passage add the Hoopoe medallion to the pool, next to the Nightingale.

Discussion question: How is the Hoopoe different than the Nightingale? Why is the Hoopoe leading the other birds on their journey?

PARROT

The parrot stepped forward and said, "I am the Khidr (as) of all the birds and desire the water of immortality."

The Hoopoe replied, "Foolish parrot, you wear the robe of green but you are not worthy of the robe of Khidr (as). You will not achieve your true quest by seeking the water of life but by following with us on the way to the Pool of Paradise, the true source of all waters and all life."

"Come dear Parrot come and see if you can follow us beyond the junction of the Sea of Mercy and the Sea of Wrath, beyond the sinking boat of this life, the crumbled wall of our civilization, and beyond the sacrifice we all must make when we submit our Will to the Will of our creator and slay our own ego. Come with us Parrot and see if you can even reach as high as our master Musa (as) before ever claiming to be like the unknowable yet all knowing Khidr (as). This life is a snare that all birds must escape to reach our real life. Bid farewell to this false life dear Parrot and follow us to the ends of this earth."

The parrot lowered his head to the ground, submitted and followed the Hoopoe on the journey.

LESSON PLAN

After reviewing the passage the child will add the Parrot medallion to the pool next to the Hoopoe.

Discussion questions: what is the mistake that the Parrot makes? How does the Hoopoe help the Parrot?

PEACOCK

The Peacock came and laid his carpet of feathers before the company.

"Do not envy my beauty for I am cursed by my own action. I am not worthy to reach to the Simourgh but I wish to return to his paradise because it is I that carried Iblis into Paradise."

The Hoopoe spoke to the Peacock, "Your True Home is beyond even the paradise you know and is more blessed and more beautiful if you can reach it. Adam (as) was not exiled for a simple sin but because Our Creator does not wish us to love His Paradise, His Creation, or any other thing he has created more than Him. We must all guard against this error and seek only the Simourgh and not the comforts of Paradise."

"The Lady Rabia knew this well and she carried a vessel of water to extinguish the fires of Hell and a torch to burn Paradise to teach us that our goal is the pleasure of our Lord and not to avoid the discomfort of Hell or seek the pleasures of Paradise."

The peacock lowered his head folded his tail and followed the Hoopoe on the journey.

LESSON PLAN

After you review the story of the Peacock your child will attach the Peacock medallion to the pool, next to the Parrot.

Discussion Questions: Why does the Peacock want to return to Paradise? Why is it better to desire the presence of God (swt) than Paradise?

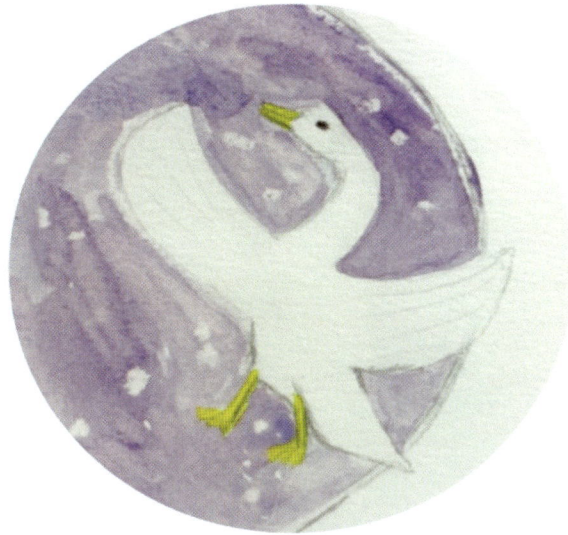

DUCK

The Duck swept up from the pond and claimed that it was clean and pure as the water dripping from its feathers. She said, "I cannot leave the water for it is my home and I am well suited to it and not at all suited to this journey before you. Leave me in my little pond and I will be content."

The Hoopoe replied, "This pond is not your home dear Duck for your home is the Pool of Paradise. If you join us in our quest you will find truer water than this and will arrive cleaner than if you remain here. All life comes from the true water in the Pool of Paradise and not the shadow of water here in this life. You cannot be clean and pure by denying our quest. And remember that the Sea of Wrath sent in the time of Nuh (as) is there, but above it is the Sea of Mercy. From which sea do you wish to take your part?"

The duck lowered her head, submitted and followed the Hoopoe on the journey.

LESSON PLAN

After reading the passage about the Duck have your child attach the Duck medallion to the pool, next to the Peacock.

Discussion questions: Are we supposed to stay where things are easy and comfortable all our lives or are we supposed to challenge ourselves with things that are difficult? In which body of water in Paradise do you think the Duck would like to live?

PARTRIDGE

The Partridge seeks precious stones and hopes to find a diamond. The Partridge said, "Because of the weight of these stones I will not be able to make the journey." The Hoopoe reprimanded the Partridge and said, "Your heart would be stone as well if you continue to seek colored stones instead of a jewel of real value."

The Hoopoe warned the Partridge, "Even Sulayman (as) was weighed down by the weight of his ring and its stone. On the day that Sulayman (as) forgot to mention his Lord upon removing the ring and its stone it was lost to him, taken by the Jinn Sakhir. This Jinn held the ring for forty days and Sulayman (as) was brought low. Each day he took two fish from the sea. One he ate the other he gave to the poor. When the Jinn was exposed as an imposter he flew away dropping the ring into the sea where it was swallowed by a fish. When Sulayman (as) took his fish to eat that night he found his ring again. Do not forget your Lord my Partridge, for Sulayman (as) was my master and my teacher and even he stumbled for the sake of a stone in a ring."

The Partridge lowered his head, submitted and followed the Hoopoe on the journey.

LESSON PLAN

After reading the passage about the Partridge have your child attach the Partridge medallion to the pool, next to the Duck.

Discussion questions: Why did Sulayman (as) lose his ring when he forgot God (swt)? Why does the Partridge want to stay with his jewels rather than go on the journey?

HUMAY

The Humay is the maker of kings. Where the shadow of the Humay falls a king is found. The Humay claims that he has no need of the Simourgh because he keeps noble company as he is. The Hoopoe reprimanded the Humay for his pride and reminded him that he must seek his real king.

The Hoopoe told the Humay the tale of the Sultan and the Dervish. "A Dervish had a dream where the Sultan cursed the Humay because he wished to be a slave of his Lord and not a king on the earth. The sultan knew God (swt) to be the true king of all the creation."

The Hoopoe continued, "If the truly noble curse you Humay and wish to find the Simourgh then what is your worth Humay? You but delay the true ambition of our assembly who seek the true king. Follow us to Mount Qaf, pass the seven valleys to the throne of your Lord. God (swt) is the maker of kings and their stories. And so it was with Daoud (as), Sulayman (as) and Dhul Qarnain (as). Where were you when they were made?"

The Humay dropped his wings low and sagged like a buzzard mumbling that it twas true and turned to follow the company of the Hoopoe.

LESSON PLAN

After reading the passage about the Humay have your child attach the medallion for the Humay to the pool, next to the Partridge.

Discussion questions: What was the challenge of the Humay bird? How did the Hoopoe convince the Humay to participate in the journey?

HAWK

The Hawk claims that he is pleased serving his king and has no need of the Simourgh. The Hoopoe tells the Hawk that a king of the earth cannot compare to the King of Creation and that he should give no value to the material world. The Hoopoe told the Hawk a story of an earthly king's fickle favor.

"One king had a servant that he used to hold an apple for target practice on his head. This servant knew the truth, that the king was mortal and might kill him with the arrow if it missed the apple. I warn you dear Hawk heed the lesson of this servant and do not forget your true master. If you come and find your true king you will be in the company of greater leaders than you will find resting here on earth."

The Hawk bowed low with his wings outstretched before their leader and his head turned toward their horizon as he followed the company.

LESSON PLAN

After reading the passage about the Hawk have the child add the Hawk medallion to the pool, next to the Humay.

Discussion questions: How are the Humay and the Hawk similar? How are they different?

HERON

The Heron claims that he is too weak to make the journey and he only desires to be near the water. The Hoopoe warns the Heron of the perils of the sea. The Hoopoe then told a tale of a Dervish who asked the Sea why it boiled and rolled and took the color blue. The Sea said it wore blue for mourning the Beloved and rolled and boiled with love for the One. The truest desire of the Sea was to have one drop of divine water from the river Kawthar, the river of paradise.

"Do not seek the Sea of this world dear Heron. Seek the Pool of Paradise that is fed by the river Kawthar, which runs to the Sea of Mercy that lies beyond the Sidratul Muntaha. As we journey to the Pool of Paradise do not forget the Isra wal Miraj. The journey to the divine presence is farther than we can imagine, but if our path is folded the road is not long."

"The night that the Prophet (sws) ascended to the heavens he was shown the river Kawthar that flows from Paradise. The angel woke him in the night. The Buraq carried him into the night. He passed the White Rooster calling all to prayer, the Tree of Life, the Door of Hell, the Sea of Wrath, the Scale of Souls, the Bayt al-Mamur, the Lote Tree, and the Sea of Mercy until he reached the river bank of Paradise. The Prophet (sws) will gather his Umma there at the Pool of Kawthar. Come dear Heron, don't delay. Come with us to the shore of the Pool of Paradise. This river is nothing but a shadow of our goal."

The Heron lifted his long legs from the water and followed the company on their journey.

LESSON PLAN

After reading the passage about the Heron have your child add the Heron medallion to the pool, next to the Humay.

Discussion questions: When the Heron does not want to go on the journey how does the Hoopoe convince him that there is a better place to go? Many of the birds in our tale do not want to leave the water. Why is that?

OWL

The owl that should be wise was a fool. He claimed that the Simourgh was a worthy goal but wished to remain in the ruins of this world with its hidden treasures buried beneath their crumbled walls.

The Hoopoe cried, "Forget not Musa (as) who heard the word of our Lord upon the mountain while his brother Harun (as) pleaded with them all. Look not to gold or the golden calf for your place of safety. Who is it that delivered you from Egypt? Who drowned Pharaoh and threw him up upon the shore? Who is it that brought you through the Red Sea? Who brought you whole to the shade of this mountain? An Idol cannot do that. The treasure of this world can bring you no safety, no security, no life. Be wise dear owl and search with us to find the real treasure at the end of our road. Do not light here in search of false idols."

The Owl closed his eyes slowly and bowed his head to the greater wisdom of the Hoopoe and turned to join their company.

LESSON PLAN

After reading the passage about the Owl have your child add the Owl medallion to the pool, next to the Heron.

Discussion questions: why does the Owl want treasures more than anything? How does the Hoopoe convince the Owl to leave the false treasures?

SPARROW

The sparrow claimed to lack the strength to make the journey. He said that he would never pass its trials. The Hoopoe called him false and said he must be silent and follow his true leader and not his pride. The sparrow wished to rest in the well with Yusuf (as) forever. The Sparrow could not see that Yusuf's (as) trials did not end in the well. Yaqub (as) could not be parted from Yusuf (as) but they were ripped apart just the same. Their trails only began at the well.

"Leave your will dear Sparrow in the bottom of the well. Come with us to find your real master and be joined with him as Yaqub (as) joined Yusuf (as) in mercy and tears in the land of Egypt. You will not find what you seek here."

"Yusuf (as) was the dearest favorite of his father Yaqub (as) and so his brothers were jealous. They threw him into the well and sold him as a slave telling Yaqub (as) he was dead. After many years they were reunited after many trials from their Lord. We too can be reunited with our Lord if we do not hide in a well of our own making."

The sparrow wiped his beak on the twig he sat upon and trilled in agreement before fluttering along the heels of their great company.

LESSON PLAN

After reading the passage about the Sparrow have your child add the Sparrow medallion to the pool, next the Owl.

Discussion questions: The Sparrow says he is too weak for the journey. Why is that not true? Why does the Sparrow want to hide in the well of Yusuf?

EAGLE

The Eagle spoke and asked the Hoopoe what was the value of obedience. Why should they follow the Hoopoe that was crowned as their leader?

The Hoopoe replied that when you have a true leader you are bettered by them and you must be grateful.

"If you follow your desires instead of your teacher then you are like Nimrod and Pharaoh and will be the creator of your destruction. Pharaoh drowned by his own conceit in the Red Sea and Nimrod was consumed by his own ego in the form of a mosquito. But if you find your true king he will guide you to your Lord. Do not let your will be your king. Let your will follow your true leader."

The eagle nodded in agreement. "It is true that a king does not a leader make," and turned to follow their company.

LESSON PLAN

After reading the passage about the Eagle have your child add the Eagle medallion to the pool, next to the Sparrow.

Discussion questions: Do you sometimes ask why you should obey your teacher or parent? Why is it important to follow those who know more than you do?

OSTRICH

The Ostrich spoke and said that he was fearful of the way and the distance and the fiery volcanoes. He wished to stay where he was and hide as an ostrich will do.

The Hoopoe called on the Ostrich to overcome his fear and that it was better to die in pursuit of higher things than live in cowardice.

"This road is not for cowards and you must become more than what you are to attain it. Think not that because you are ill suited to the journey you cannot achieve it. Do not forget Daoud (as) and Goliath. The believers needed a champion that could defeat the giant Goliath and they sent out young Daoud (as) with his slingshot. The three pebbles found their mark and the giant was defeated. We must find our mark and not be swayed by fear or delay."

The Ostrich thumped the ground hard with his heavy foot and then turned to follow the Hoopoe.

LESSON PLAN

After reading the passage about the Ostrich have your child add the Ostrich medallion to the pool, next to the Eagle.

Discussion questions: What do Ostrich birds do when they are afraid? Why is it not helpful to hide when you are afraid of a challenge? Why does the Hoopoe speak about the bravery of Daoud (as) to the Ostrich?

LOVEBIRD

The Lovebird cooed and folded her wings beside her. He said that he was a sinner and inconstant in spirit except in love.

"I sometimes love so much that all else disappears. It tis a sin, is it not, to love another more than God (swt). How can I love God (swt) more than all else so that I might make the journey from love rather than obligation?"

The Hoopoe spoke, "The Lady Zulaikha loved Yusuf (as) so much that she forgot all other things. Your love does not disqualify you any more than it disqualified her, but we must first remember God. Remember that your Lord created the one you love. You are asked to love and remember your Lord as well because without your Lord you would have nothing to love."

The Dove cooed in agreement and unwound her wings to follow her heart to Mount Qaf.

LESSON PLAN

After reading the passage about the Lovebird have your child add the Lovebird medallion to the pool, next to the Ostrich.

Discussion questions: Why does the Lovebird want to love God (swt)? How does the Lovebird use his love to find his motivation?

SEAGULL

The Seagull spoke and claimed that he was a thief by nature and how can a thief make this journey?

The Hoopoe warned the Seagull not to allow his will to steal his own destiny. The true thief is the will; it robs you of all that you have toiled to acquire.

"The Mullah, Nasruddin, was sleeping in his home one night when his wife woke him to say there was a thief in the house. Nusruddin did not seem concerned and said that it was not any great matter for they had nothing in the home worth stealing. His wife did not agree with this and finally Nasruddin said that if the thief were to find something of value in the house this would be a good thing because then he (Nasruddin) could take it from the thief."

"When you live as a dervish it is true that there will be little you own worth stealing for the true treasures that you hold are not the things that can be taken from your house."

The Seagull cawed to all that they should come and turned to follow the Hoopoe.

LESSON PLAN

After reading the passage about the Seagull have your child add the Seagull medallion to the pool, next to the Lovebird.

Discussion questions: This is the second bird who claims that a flawed individual must somehow be disqualified from making the journey but how does the Hoopoe use their flaws to encourage them? If someone did bad things does that mean they cannot use their talents to do good?

FLAMINGO

The Flamingo swished forward and tucked his leg under his breast. I am too beautiful to be ruined by a long and dangerous journey.

"You are truly the Bird of Vanity," scolded the Hoopoe, and he went on.

"Vanity of vanities! All is vanity.
All streams run to the sea,
but the sea is not full;
to the place where the streams flow,
 there they flow again.
the eye is not satisfied with seeing,
What has been is what will be,
and what has been done is what will be done,
and there is nothing new under the sun."
(Ecclisiastes)

"So if you should think yourself special and unique dear Flamingo then think again."

The Flamingo was shamed and then said that he was afraid of sorrow and pain and sacrifice.

So the Hoopoe said,

"For in much wisdom is much vexation,
 and he who increases knowledge increases sorrow." (Ecclesiastes)

"It is so that the wise will know the hour of their death and be somber thereafter. But you should be more somber still for you know not the hour of yours or the reward that you will lose in your next life through your ignorance."

The Flamingo lowered his head and unwound his foot to follow upon the tail feathers of the Hoopoe to the Pool of Paradise.

LESSON PLAN

After reading the passage about the Flamingo have your child add the Flamingo medallion to the pool, next to the Seagull.

Discussion questions: What is the ego of the Flamingo? Are we also afraid of pain and sacrifice? How does Shaitan try to trick us out of connection with the Divine?

WOODPECKER

The Woodpecker lighted on the perch and tap taped for all attention. "I am accused of hoarding my wealth in this world and not sharing but I say that I cannot risk losing all I've worked so hard to acquire and this journey seems too dangerous to me."

The Hoopoe said, "You must remember the loyal companion of the Prophet...Abu Bakr (r) who gave all his worldly wealth and lost noting from it. He kept not one coin for himself and his generosity has been handsomely rewarded by his Lord."

"Forget not the spider that covered the cave of Hira with its web. The web is the world, the fly is your sustenance. Be not content to rest on a web forever but fly with us to the ends of creation."

The Woodpecker tap tapped in agreement and turned to follow the company.

LESSON PLAN

After reading the passage about the Woodpecker have your child add the Woodpecker medallion to the pool, next to the Flamingo.

Discussion questions: Why does the Woodpecker want to stay in the world? How does the Hoopoe convince the Woodpecker that true security is with God (swt)?

GOLDFINCH

The goldfinch fluttered to the perch and cried, "I am afraid to make this journey because I fear the flame of desire. I have come close to the sun before and so took my flame yellow feathers. I wish to go with you to join the one whom my soul loves but I have been burnt before. We will follow you dear Hoopoe on the tracks of the flock."

The Hoopoe spoke, "Ayyoub (as) withstood many trials and his love for God (swt) did not diminish. He was wealthy and prosperous with many things to be thankful for and Shaitan whispered that Ayyoub (as) only loved God (swt) because of his good fortune. God (swt) sent much hardship and pain to Ayyoub (as) to see if this was true and his love did not diminish. Our Lord knows that there are three kinds of believers: one that comes near the flame of love and is warmed by the love of God. Another touches the flame and is burnt by the love of God. And the last will throw themselves into the flame in fanah (annihilation). If we are to succeed in our quest we must desire the presence of our Lord as Ayyoub (as) and not fear the flames."

The Goldfinch trilled loudly and rose up into the light of the moon until she disappeared for a moment in the bright light before sinking slowly to her branch and turning to follow their company.

LESSON PLAN

After reading the passage about the Goldfinch have your child add the Goldfinch medallion to the pool, next to the Woodpecker.

Discussion questions: Why does the Goldfinch want to make the journey even though he fears the fire? How does the Hoopoe explain the flame of God's (swt) love?

TURTLEDOVE

The Turtledove cooed and said, "In the early morning I sing my song with a sad heart. I saw the flood of Nuh. I brought the olive branch. My feet were washed in the Sea of Wrath and I fear to be in peril again. I will come with you. I will obey but I fear death as I have seen it, as much death as can been seen."

The Hoopoe said, "Have strength dear dove as you are worthy through your service to Nuh (as)! Be like the phoenix and rise from your own ashes, the pyre of your rebirth. We that are born will die and remember that it is the eternal life that we seek and our true safety is from our Lord. When we arrive together in Jannah we will see that there is indeed the Sea of Wrath, but above it and still larger is the endless Sea of Mercy. On its shore you will reside in a windblown tree, your feathers bleached white by the sun. In your beak you shall hold the tiny black pebble holding all our sins and when your Lord bids you drop it to the water..."

"The Lord shall say:

You are the nation of Muhammad (sws).
Within the pebble are the errors of his nation,
and this sea is my mercy upon you all."

"You who have witnessed and survived the Sea of Wrath shall spend eternity
on the shores of the Sea of Mercy dear dove, beyond the Lote Tree near to
the presence of your Lord and you are so honored."

The Hoopoe bowed low to honor the dove above the others of their company
and all the others followed.

The dove shed a tear and cooed, "Nuh (as) had told me this was so and I had
forgotten. Let us follow the Hoopoe to the ends of this earth for all we do here
is error and forget all that is worth remembering."

LESSON PLAN

After reading the passage about the Turtledove have your child add the
Turtledove medallion to the pool, next to the Goldfinch.

Discussion questions: Why did the dove fear death? Why is the dove honored
for his service to Nuh (as)?

EGRET

The Egret twirled before the company with wings outstretched like a dervish and then folded them and bowed.

"When I turn I am with the sun and travel the seven tracts through the sky in great company. Why should one that journeys the sky as I do seek to travel farther?"

The Hoopoe said, "Dear Egret, you must learn humility if you are to succeed. We must learn from the Prophet Muhammad (sws). One day he was offered a bunch of grapes by a poor and sincere man and the Prophet (sws) ate every single one. When later asked why he did not share this gift he said that the grapes were sour and he did not want the man to be shy that his gift was not sweet."

"You go round and round in circles like an ambitious bat with no direction. Whirl dear dervish of the birds if you must, but you will not ascend if your heart is not still and steadfast in your chest. You cannot seek the sun if you are blind. While you whirl your heart must be still."

The Egret twirled round and round toward their horizon and followed the Hoopoe.

LESSON PLAN

After reading the passage about the Egret have your child add the Egret medallion to the pool, next to the Turtledove.

Discussion questions: What is the ego of the Egret? The Egret is known as the whirling dervish bird; what are we supposed to do when we whirl?

RAVEN

The raven lighted, straight and sleek, folding his shiny black feathers tightly beside him.

"I am resigned to the journey yet suffrage is for a purpose but suffering is not. I fear I will not be among those that survive this journey and so what will become of us who persevere yet fail to reach the end?"

The Hoopoe said, "We all end the same and leave the world in death. Do not forget that each day we choose to follow our Lord or we choose to listen to the whispers of Iblis (Satan). Ayyub (as) suffered long and terribly yet did not despair, for his love of God (swt) depended not upon his good fortune on this earth. Iblis said that the love of Ayyub (as) would not withstand his trials but it did. Ayyub (as) was blessed with prosperity and followers and good health. When all these blessings disappeared he was struck down with a terrible affliction of the skin. He lost everything but his wife Rahma (r) and was cast out by the people. After a time of trial he was cured and he and his wife were restored to youth and health by a fountain of water. Do not forget that he succeeded in resisting Iblis, that his prosperity was restored and his faith rewarded. So it shall be with you all in life as well as death if you take the prophets as your guides and do not loose your way."

"I have ever been the one to follow one step behind death, and so I shall follow the Hoopoe," and the Raven turned to join their company.

LESSON PLAN

After reading the passage about the Raven have your child add the Raven medallion to the pool, next to the Egret.

Discussion questions: The Raven asked what was the fate of those who died on the quest; what do you think will happen to them? How did the Hoopoe answer the Raven?

PENGUIN

The penguin waddled forward slowly.

"I can walk the path but I cannot fly it. I ask to be blessed with sincerity on this way as my own earthbound condition is comical even to me among this winged company."

The Hoopoe addressed the Penguin, "Oh Penguin, you who stand for long cold months, holding your precious egg aloft take heart. Just as the spring will come and the egg will hatch you will see the journey's end on your long march to the Sea of Mercy. This path will not appear to all who seek but will open to the ones who are strong and do not waver in the winter wind. You will be like the Magicians who followed Musa (as) and his second mother Asiya (r). They stood firm upon the foundation of their faith despite horrible trials and suffering and you shall see when you arrive with us the reward they enjoy now that they are at peace."

The Penguin bowed as elegantly as he could and turned to follow their company.

LESSON PLAN

After reading the passage about the Penguin have your child add the Penguin medallion to the pool, next to the Raven.

Discussion questions: How does the Penguin use his Will to overcome his physical limitations? Have you ever had trouble doing something physical? A long walk? Lifting something heavy? Swimming? How did you solve this problem?

WAGTAIL

The Wagtail perched and rolled, balancing its long tail and said, "This is a worthy cause and I direct my will to achieve our goal. Please dear Hoopoe tell us how we can aspire to reach our goal. What focus should we make? On what should we meditate to achieve success?"

The Hoopoe said, "You must be like Musa (as) upon Mount Sanai. You must see the fire in the desert. You must remember he who went from slave to the Prince of Egypt was so blessed with a purpose."

"We must all acquire wings and escape the locked chest of life so that when the lid is lifted upon our death we might escape. We must have wings of the spirit like our dear Penguin and take flight."

The Wagtail bowed low with a swish of his tail and followed.

LESSON PLAN

After reading the passage about the Wagtail have your child add the Wagtail medallion to the pool, next to the Penguin.

Discussion questions: When the Wagtail asked the Hoopoe for inspiration what did he say? What do you do when you want to be inspired to achieve a goal?

FALCON

The Noble Falcon folded his wings high above the company and dove sharply. He lifted his wings before them and swooped down to the perch before the other birds.

"My Will chooses the path of justice and so I follow the Hoopoe. I ask you dear Hoopoe to tell us how the just are informed by spiritual wisdom so that we may discern true justice from false when a judgment is used to oppress and not to protect the weak and innocent."

The Hoopoe addressed the company, "True justice is with our Lord. Some will see justice in this dunya (earth) and some only in akhira (heaven). When Yusuf (as) was separated from his father Yaqub (as) they grieved but they trusted in God's justice and they were reunited and the brothers of Yusuf (as) were exposed for their jealousy and forgiven. The cup of Yusuf (as) spoke and reveled the crime of his brothers, but they had sinned against themselves. Yusuf (as) was in this life twice imprisoned, once in the well and once in Egypt and he was delivered twice and raised high for his trust in God's judgment."

"Remember dear hawk that justice is better than vengeance and that to God (swt) one that begs for his justice is better than a scholar that theorizes about justice."

The Noble Falcon tilted his head in agreement with the Hoopoe and lifted his wing to point the way.

LESSON PLAN

After reading the passage about the Falcon have your child add the Falcon medallion to the pool, next to the Wagtail.

Discussion questions: The Falcon asked what is real justice, what do you think real justice is? Why does the Falcon ask about real justice? Why is justice important?

CROW

The crow lighted with a clamorous flapping of wings nearly toppling the perch and asked if boldness was a crucial component of courage for the journey at hand. "For I am full of boldness," he said, "but less so of wisdom by some measure."

The Hoopoe said, "A true sage is bold from certainty of purpose and the support of God (swt). Dhul-Qarnian (as) conquered the known world upon the shoulders of his certainty. If he can reach to the ends of this earth than so can we. He traveled and conquered even the great monsters Gog and Magog and locked them up behind a wall of lead and iron where they are imprisoned to this day."

"Your courage may yet save you from the curse laid upon you by Nuh (as) for your faithless service after the flood. You were sent abroad by the prophet to search for dry land and became distracted by a carcass left by the flood. Do not become distracted on our journey or no quantity of boldness or courage will correct your intention again."

The crow bowed his head in shame.

"It is so!" he said. "Keep me on the straight path and not the path of those who go astray."

LESSON PLAN

After reading the passage about the Crow have your child add the Crow medallion to the pool, next to the Falcon.

Discussion questions: What is the fault of the Crow? Do you think the Crow will stay on the path and not become distracted like he did after the flood? Have you ever forgotten to do something important? Have you ever had an experience where you had to be bold and brave?

SWAN

The swan glided forward upon a pond of glass and ripples spread by his wings. The swan claimed to love the Simourgh of the Caucasus but it was himself that he loved and not his true king.

He said, "If the Simourgh loves me as I love the Simourgh then he cannot want me to be spoiled by this journey into a disheveled carcass. If the Simourgh loves us truly he cannot want the hardships of the journey but only sweetness and ease."

The Hoopoe said, "Do not have love of yourself or this world dear swan. Any form you have here in dunya is a shadow of the true form you will have at the shore of the Pool of Paradise. Even if the journey burns away every feather you will be better for it. Remember that the beauty of Zulaykha (r) and the beauty of Rahma (r) was restored after their trials. Zulaykha (r) loved Yusuf (as) and she was rewarded with marriage to him and her youth returned. He found her old and living in the streets of Egypt but when her prayer was answered she became young and beautiful once more and bore Yusuf (as) 11 sons."

"Rahma (r) was restored by the fountain that healed Ayyoub (as). She and her husband were cast out and lived in poverty for a time. Rahma (r) stayed with her husband and did not abandon him."

"Your beauty is of no value if you do not reach your goal and one day soon the fire of time will burn your plume away until there is nothing left and you will be hollow, not because you have lost your beauty but because you have wronged your soul."

The Swan covered her beak with her wing to conceal her tears before turning to join the flock.

LESSON PLAN

After reading the passage about the Swan have your child add the Swan medallion to the pool, next to the Crow.

Discussion questions: What is the ego problem of the Swan? When God (swt) sends us challenges is that good or bad? Have you ever wanted to look nice rather than to work hard?

CUCKOO

The Cuckoo bobbled slowly on the perch and enumerated all of his many accomplishments and asked why after having already worked so hard he should join a harsh and dangerous journey.

The Hoopoe spoke and reprimanded that Cuckoo for his laziness. He told the tale where Musa (as) was sent by God (swt) to take the advice of Iblis. Iblis cautioned Musa (as) to avoid saying "I" and to beware your dragons of pride or one day you will be like me, destroyed by my ego and a thief of my own soul.

The Cuckoo tilted his head in agreement and turned to follow the Hoopoe.

LESSON PLAN

After reading the passage about the Cuckoo have your child add the Cuckoo medallion to the pool, nest to the Swan.

Discussion questions: What was the ego problem of the Cuckoo? How did the Hoopoe help the Cuckoo to overcome this problem? Have you ever refused to do something important because you thought you already did enough? How did you overcome this problem?

BLUE JAY

The Blue Jay floated down like a slice of sky and lighted on the perch and asked, "What should I ask the Simourgh?

The Hoopoe then told them that God (swt) once asked Daoud (as) if any would search for their Lord without fear of Hell or promise of Heaven. It is in the stories of our guides that we find the most worthy questions. How can you know the secret if you are in need of Paradise and fear Hell? He was told that he should seek only his Lord.

Rabia (q) knew that to desire the gardens or to fear the fire makes us hypocrites so we shall leave this world behind and carry the pitcher of water to put out the fires of hell and the torch to burn heaven so that it is our Lord alone we seek.

The Blue Jay lifted each wing as though she held the torch and bucket and turned to follow the Hoopoe.

LESSON PLAN

After reading the passage about the Blue Jay have your child add the Blue Jay medallion to the pool, next to the Cuckoo.

Discussion questions: What do you think the Blue Jay will ask the Simourgh? Why is the presence of God (swt) better than Paradise? If you were a bird on this journey what would you ask?

GOOSE

The Goose waddled forward and asked, "What gift shall I bring my king?"

The Goose thought to bring its golden eggs but the Hoopoe said that the Simourgh desires that which does not exist there upon Mount Qaf. The Simourgh desires your ardent love not your blind obedience. Come to the Simourgh as Zulaykha (r) came to Yusuf (as).

The Goose then said, "I who have traveled far upon this earth do know that the road before us is far. How can we hope to close such a long distance?"

The Hoopoe said, "There are 7 valleys. Dear Goose your greatest strength is your greatest folly. You have travelled farther on this earth than any other it is true but this journey is not only a question of distance but question of resolve. When the Prophet Muhammad (sws) and Abu Bakr (ra) travelled for Mecca to Medina it was more than just distance they travelled. They were leaving their home. They were pursued by those who wanted to kill them. Before their journey and after their journey is a marker for all time."

The Goose nodded for it was so and swung to follow the Hoopoe.

LESSON PLAN

After reading the passage about the Goose have your child add the Goose medallion to the pool, next to the Blue Jay.

Discussion questions: What is the ego problem of the Goose? Have you ever been afraid to go somewhere because it was too far? Were you surprised after that the road seemed shorter than you thought?

PIGEON

The Pigeon bobbled forward and addressed the company. "Some say that to find the Simourgh you must come as a beggar. Myself and my flock are the beggar birds of this earth. We come to the Simourgh with our begging bowl empty and ready to be filled with divine love and knowledge. Tell us dear Hoopoe how the poor and stupid can come to the Simourgh or are we too low to make such a great journey."

The Hoopoe said, "Pigeon you have the faith to follow Khidr (as). Not all the learned or high can follow this teacher. Few understand his lessons or can bear his tests for long. You who have lived low on this earth and have no love of dunya have naught to lose but your souls. Khidr (as) leads both Prophets and Saints on this earth to a truer knowledge than most can bear. You are indeed worthy and you may give your greetings to Khidr (as) on our way for he still walks the earth on the orders of his Lord."

The Pigeon chortled with glee and bobbled quickly after the Hoopoe and his great company.

LESSON PLAN

After reading the passage about the Pigeon have your child add the Pigeon medallion to the pool, next to the Goose.

Discussion questions: What was the question of the Pigeon? Have you ever felt that you were not smart enough or high enough to do something great? Why is it difficult to follow Khidr (as)?

THE VALLEY OF HUNGER

The valley of hunger has many faces. In English the morning meal is called the break-fast meaning that we have spent the night without food or drink. In Ramadan this is reversed and we fast from morning to night rather than night to morning. Some believe that when we sleep we leave our bodies and travel back to our Lord and during this journey we fast. The birds that follow the Hoopoe in this tale pass through 7 valleys on their way to their Lord and their transport for the journey is their hunger for the divine.

VALLEY OF THE QUEST

If you want to reach the Pool of Paradise you must be brave and bold and quick as the one who conquered Goliath. He shed his armor and relied on his Lord. When Daoud (as) faced the giant he defeated him with three pebbles and a sling shot. The three pebbles found their mark and struck Goliath in the head killing him. The army of believers were victorious because of the swiftness and bravery of Daoud (as). God (swt) blessed Daoud (as) with a beautiful voice to attract the animals. The wild creatures below in the valley are his followers and they give us salaam and bid us give their salaam to Daoud (as) in Paradise.

VALLEY OF LOVE

When they came upon the next valley they found the river Nile winding before them with papyrus along its banks. When Sayyidina Yusuf came here he had many trials. He was a slave; he was thrown in prison; he was raised to great power and through it all he was loved by the Lady Zulaykha. We must be like Lady Zulaykha and pursue the Simourgh as she chased Yusef (as) through the Valley of Love. The Nile bids us salaam and asks us to greet the Prophet Yusuf (as) when we reach the Pool of Paradise.

VALLEY OF UNDERSTANDING

The Prophet Muhammad (sws) said "Seek knowledge even if you must travel to China." Today we see the Valley of Understanding below us and we seek that knowledge.

After the believers made the Exodus out of Egypt Sayyidina Musa sought greater knowledge with Khidr (as) at the place where the river and the fish were joined again. Khidr (as) told Musa (as) that his knowledge was not for Musa (as) but they travelled together for a time. Khidr (as) drilled holes in the boat that carried them, struck a young boy dead, and rebuilt a falling wall, but Musa (as) was not able to understand why. Khidr (as) tried to share his knowledge with Musa (as) but he did not see until he was told that the boat was to be stolen and was saved by the minor damage; the boy was to be a tyrant and his believing parents were saved from misery; the wall concealed a treasure belonging to orphans that would have been stolen if Khidr (as) had left the wall in ruin. Khidr (as) still walks the earth. He bids us salaam and asks us to greet Musa (as) when we reach the Pool of Paradise.

VALLEY OF DETACHMENT

The Prophet (sws) bids us seek knowledge even if we must go to China but the pursuit of knowledge did not begin in China. It began below in the Valley of Eden. God (swt) taught Adam (as) the names of all things including the Tree of Knowledge which he was told not to touch. Iblis whispered to Adam (as) and Eve (ra) and told them that they would perish if they did not eat of the wheat tree and so they ate and were cast out of the garden. We must seek knowledge and the understanding to use it well or it will destroy us on our road to the Pool of Paradise. The Tree of Knowledge bids us salaam and asks us to send regards to Adam (as).

Every moment on this earth our souls are in exile and those who know are in mourning. Adam(as) knew this when he fell to earth and left the garden. And lo we have arrived at a blessed place but we are not yet done.

VALLEY OF UNITY

In the valley below you can see the Sidratul Muntaha (Lote Tree) glowing with the light of angels. The Prophet (sws) ascended through the heavens on Isra wal Miraj and he came to this tree. Beyond it he was united with the presence of his Lord and so we find ourselves in the Valley of Unity.

The Prophet (sws) came to this place of unity and then returned to tell the tale. What a tale you shall tell your chicks and goslings one day!

VALLEY OF ASTONISHMENT

In the night Musa (as) saw the acacia tree did not burn yet was full of flames. We live in a dream yet Musa (as) awoke in this valley and heard the voice of God (swt). We have nearly arrived so take heart.

VALLEY OF DEATH

When the Prophet Idris (as) ascended he saw the
Sirat ul Mustaqueem and the darkness that lay below.

The purpose of the trials on this journey is to strengthen the consciousness
with the will so that there is a tempered soul that survives the trial of death. We
are not what we were when we started our journey.

THE POOL OF PARADISE

On this day when the 6 days of Shawal have ended we have reached the Pool of Paradise. The birds looked into the pool and they did not find their reflection but the longer they looked the more clearly they saw a golden light take form. The form was that of the Simourgh their king and leader who slowly vanished before their eyes and there were no more birds and no more Simourgh and no more pool and only the light of God (swt) remained.

Please see our other books on Amazon now.

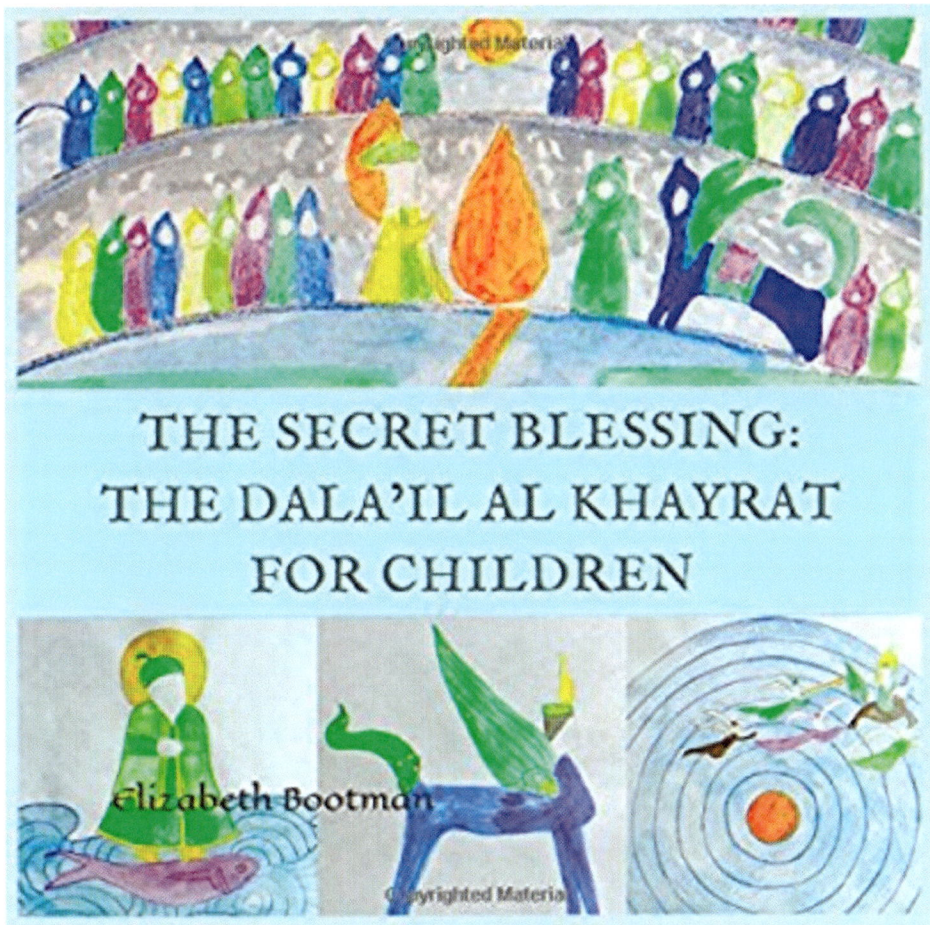

THE SECRET BLESSING:
THE DALA'IL AL KHAYRAT
FOR CHILDREN

Elizabeth Bootman

Printed in Great Britain
by Amazon